Mad Dog
and Maria

A Beginner's Guide to Greatness

By

Stern Ern

Published by

Etica Press Ltd·
147 Worcester Road
Malvern
Worcestershire
WR14 1ET

© Etica Press Ltd 2005

A CIP Catalogue record for this book is available from the British Library.

ISBN 10: 1-905633-00-9
ISBN 13: 978-1-905633-00-5

Printed by Pear Tree Press Ltd, Stevenage, Herts SG1 2PT

www.eticapress.com

For my mum and dad.
Thank you for everything.
I love you always.

My father often told me
You don't know until you try.
How right he was

As usual my mother looked on
and smiled.
That meant get on with it.

Intro ...

As a thirty something I thought that I had better put pen to paper and do something. Being a very late thirty something and due to the annoying saying of 'everybody has a least one book in them' here goes.

After all, thanks to yet another similarly annoying phrase, my life begins with my next birthday.

I used to think that the only way I would ever have a book in me would be if I ate one but thanks to my beautiful wife, what you are about to feast your eyes on is that very book. No, not the one that I may or may not have tried to eat, and no my wife did not write the following pages.

The unswerving belief that Nicky (my wife) has in me has led me to this. So once again here goes.

Confused yet? No?

Give it time then. I'm good at this.

Hello. Ern's the name and stern is the game. What I hear you cry. Surely not. My wife tells me that although I am cute and cuddly I have an evil face. In fact some of the descriptions that have come my way lead me to believe that maybe my horns were cut off at birth!

With reference to the cuddly bit, let it be known that the love of a good woman not forgetting the large portions at mealtimes now mean that I enter a room belly first.

But I must admit that I am now digressing from the point in hand and that my dear readers happens to be the title of the book. The Mad Dog in question happens to be my father and the Maria is of course my wonderful mother. Henceforth, though, they shall be known as mum and dad. The other words are very formal, very British and in my opinion for the posh people of which I am not one. It's also all bollocks!

I must now caution you dear reader. I do have the odd opinion about a great many things and I have been known on occasion to express myself.

So you may find as you go on that I wander off the beaten track a bit but, have no fear, once the rant has ended then the ramblings can continue. Now where was I?

Oh yes.

The reason for what you are about to read is my mum and dad. On our last trip to Holland, which is where they live, my wife and I were fortunate enough to be given two caricature drawings of them both.

In truth I blagged them before my sisters could get them! Tough shit I say and why not. Should have been quicker and that's that.

Have to let them know what I've written in here now or they won't speak to me ever again. Then again I'll give that some thought.

Anyway back to the pictures. They were drawn by a street artist in Norway in 1974 . Having had such a good week with them and while on the ferry on our return journey I turned to my wife and told her that I was going to write a book about my mum and dad and what I was going to call it. Having at present one third of a turd of a fantasy novel in the works I did express my concern at how good this one would be

And I quote.

'I know you can do it. I have every faith in you poppet.' Unquote. We shall return to 'poppet' later.

And I can still remember the look on Nicky's face when I uttered my most famous of sayings.

'It's ok. I have a plan!'

Right then ..

James William Platt (my dad) married Maria Filomena Cornoldi in September 1964. The 19th to be precise just in case you thought that I had forgotten. They were married in Salisbury Cathedral in Rhodesia which is a country that no longer goes by that name. This is due to the ever decreasing British empire. Which while I'm on the subject, where my mum was born, Malawi, was a British protectorate. Why? Protecting who from whom. In my opinion, of which I have many, this is yet another glaring example of the British thinking that they can wander in and do what they like. As long that is if there is reasonable backing from the Americans. But I'm losing the plot here and that is a debate that can rage at another time.

So, my parents got married. They have been together for over forty years now which explains my age. My dad was born in the late thirties and my mum in the early forties.

This however means that they have reached a stage in their lives where they are now cool.

They are not at that age where they wish to hang on to past glories and dress like their children. (Unlike myself who has reached that age and have made myself look stupid on occasion!)

There is no embarrassment when you see them walking down the street towards you. In fact the only occasion which was funny was my dad rounding the corner on his bicycle and nearly running both my wife and myself over.

He duly gave us the house key, we thanked him and off he rode. As he went we noticed that he was still wearing his slippers.

Anyway the age thing.

Neither are they duffers who wander off to their local spar shop on pension day for a bottle of Spar special blend of whisky and forty Gold Mark cigarettes. Worse still it could be White Horse of which I have a particular dislike.

Having stocked up on the crap booze, toddle off back to the house where they can smoke themselves stupid drink like crazy then fall asleep and piss their pants.

No they have not reached that age. They are cool and therefore spending time with them is a real pleasure.

However five months after getting hitched my dad got himself another good job and they upped sticks and moved to Canada in January 1965.

Just over a year after that, in May of 1966, the hero of this tale, which you may now have guessed is me, was born.

My dad

My mum

A star is born!

Told you it was cold!

How happy we look! The birth of supermodels

Imagine if you will, and you will have to because you were not there, what it must have felt like to be a baby born into the frozen wastes of the Northern Territories of Canada. A place that is covered by a thick blanket of snow for six months of the year and is cold for the remaining six.

I have tried to imagine it also. If anyone ever tells you that they can remember when they were a baby they are either on very strong medication or mental. What is certain though is that you can guarantee that they are talking utter crap.

I've seen the baby photos and my parents have told me a bit about it but no I do not remember. That is why dear reader there are no stories to tell.

My sister (one of them) was born a year later. So now there were two of us I remember nothing. In September 1968 my parents moved back to Africa but because I have not done too much research in this area there is also nothing to tell.

And the reason for such a lack of detail? Well, in order to furnish you with the whatnots and wherefore before the time when my memory can kick itself into gear I would have to question my mum and dad.

The first that I wish them to know of this book is when I hand them a copy.

I have therefore relied on my photos which is a good enough indicator I must explain, however, what my dad did for a living. He was (was because he has now retired) a geologist. That is to say that he can look at rocks and tell you what's in them. Stuff like that.

No more kiddies were born during this time and in July 1969 my dad got an even better job and we moved to County Wicklow in southern Ireland. The place where we eventually ended up living was Dale House on the outskirts of a small village called Avoca. Better known to all and sundry as the setting for the very good and unfortunately in the end utter crap series Ballykissangel.

Can you see how my memory is slowly winding up like a great gas turbine? A few more pages and we'll be at a gallop!

Now in order to engage that gallop, fast forward three years to 1972 and the final sprog appears. So now there were three and, lo and behold, I had gained another sister.

Life in Ireland was great. Great to the point of being absolutely fucking awesome.

Dale House was tantamount to being an old farmhouse with lots of land and when I say lots, every year my dad found out that there was more and more land attached. Dad created a huge vegetable garden and of the small orchard that was there his pride and joy was a cooking apple tree of immense

Dale House

RNI 884 in front of Dale House

Crime Scene Central

**Studying the sea
around Port Isaac**

**Wiggle it ...
Just a little bit!**

proportions. Many a happy hour was spent climbing and falling out of that tree.

Heady times and from dawn until dusk a child could amuse him or herself to their hearts' content.

I do need to tell you that there is a point to all this. It's not so much about myself and my sisters growing up all over the place but about my parents and the end of this journey will ultimately be the answer to a lot of questions. Things that have been learned and things that are best forgotten. So much so that I won't even mention the things that are best forgotten.

Making any sense yet?

Keep reading and hopefully in the end you will know what I mean. Hopefully you will see in your mind's eye some of the slings and arrows that have been suffered. The odd poem is going to creep its way in and also be the odd recipe but and I must stress this. Do not attempt to recreate any of the recipes that appear in this book. They have been designed (by my mum) with the best intentions but, and you can trust me here, just the smell will make you heave. (Sorry mum. Please see witch's brews later on in the book!)

Quick story.

Aged about seven or eight I had one of those foldaway bicycles with the u-shaped handlebars. (It was Ireland and that was a cool thing for a small boy in the country.) Anyhow, in an attempt to make my bike even cooler I bagged one of my dad's spanners and flipped the handlebars down. I now had a racing bike! This was great for about a week but the bars now flipped were very low and made my back hurt. Come on. We were all kids once. Lads, you know the score.

With a bad back and the ensuing question mark posture in its infancy I reasoned to myself that it would be a good idea to put my bike back to the way, it was. Now its one thing to undo a bolt, and it's quite another to put it all back and do it, up. As it happens I was only, seven or eight and not that strong but I, did my best and it all went back, shipshape and Bristol fashion.

Imagine then the surprise I got a few days later when out biking. Having raced down a hill at what I thought to be the speed of light, I really did have the good fortune to hit a 'small rock in the road.

It was one of those lovely slow-motion moments that you have as I watched my handle bars move forward and flip neatly into their racing bike position. If there were points for the following gymnastic move that ripped me from my saddle and hurled me to the ground then I feel sure that I would have been awarded a perfect score.

I was on my own at the time so only felt stupid instead of looking it which I suppose is a bit of a blessing. My right knee was a mess and blood flowed freely as did the tears. Duly limping home my mum patched me up and my dad sorted the handlebars when he got in from work.

That, my friends, was one of the first life lessons that I got from my dad.

If it's built that way don't bugger about with it and if you do mess with it then pray before you play!

Happy families

Questions questions

Who am I?
What am I?
Why was I sent here?
It's it all a joke?
What is my purpose, my direction?
Who made me?
Where do I go, what do I do?
Questions always questions.
Always seeking the answers,
Never finding the truth.
One day I will die,
And then I shall know.

What if

What if the universe wasn't real?
What if we didn't exist?
What if it was all a joke?
Who would have the last laugh?

Told you there would be some poetry. And there's plenty more where they came from. Be aware that my mind is a veritable craphole of stunning yet some would say useless information!!

Now we need to go off the beaten track slightly because the next exciting installment is going to be about crime and punishment.

Introducing Port Issac into the frame.

Port Isaac as the name suggests is indeed a port and sits snugly on the north coast of Cornwall. It is a small and some would say (them again) picturesque village. Suffice to say that the bottom half is where the old cottages lie overlooking the harbour.

The top half looks just like any run of the mill council estate you can find the length and breadth of the country. Nevertheless, Port Isaac is where my dad was born and is a place where myself and my siblings were sent every year for a summer holiday. It is where I had my first job in the summer as a sprightly twelve year old. Washing dishes in a hotel. £1.75 an hour and as many crab claws as I could eat.

The locals were very friendly but then again we were the kids of a 'a local lad who done good.'

Hang on to your panties here as some more top Port Isaac ad lib sayings are guaranteed to crop up.

Now I'm not going to run the place down or make fun of the people who live there. It's a very close-knit community and I like it there. But then again I am me and I will say what I wish.

My parents bought a house there in the seventies. In the old part which was good. I think it was the house that he was born in but if I am wrong, and sometimes I am, it was the house next door. Close but no cigar. I know but its better than a kick up the jacksy with a size nine!

Port Issac though is the beginning of where the rot began to set in and where the first levels of expectation were laid firmly at my door. The old boys who sat on benches puffing on their rollups would tell me tales of my dad but they were also laced with menace.

'Hello my 'andsome, how are you?'

'You look just like your father.'

'He's a good chap your dad. Done Port Isaac proud.'

'Good boxer your dad, could have gone all the way.'

To clarify good boxer it would have been necessary to have spoken to his trainer whose name I forget but I chatted to him on several occasions. The man had nothing but praise for my dad and his abilities and expressed a certain sorrow that he had not gone all the way. From my point of view and from what I had been told, dear old dad was a hard fucker and could take on all comers. I have also seen the clippings from the newspapers about some of his fights, one line in particular I will never forget till the day I die.

'Platt boxed on with blood streaming down his face:'

Now I ask you. How cool is that? I'll tell you. Very cool. Quentin fucking Tarantino cool. That's how cool..

Enough swearing and enough violence. Time to get back to where the rot set in. The locals are great and they tell you things but one immortal line would be repeated to me time and time again, a line which haunts me to this day but one that I have learned to live with.

'When you grow up, if you're half the man your father is then you'll be ok.'

And bugger me didn't I give it a go.

Crime and punishment then.

By the way we're back in Ireland now.

Did you know that apart from the punishment fitting the crime in a twisted sort of way an inadvertent punishment can end in a crime? It's story time again and we will begin with Casel.

The crime involves nuts. Hazelnuts. Only Cadburys did not take these one and cover them in chocolate. (And what ever happened to the Aztec bar? Not the crappy one that came out a few years ago. The good one.) Anyway, hazelnuts.

Stashed in one corner of the grounds at Dale House was a dilapidated old shed. One end wall stood proud, most of one back wall was present and a two-brick high wall at the front. You will be surprised to hear that there was no roof.

All the wood for the fire was stacked up there and a few bits and pieces for the garden. Oh what times were had there. On one occasion dad had built a den come clubhouse for my sisters and their friends. (Some secret sect that I have no recollection of.) As chance would have it, two small boys (my friend and I) and a box of matches later and the den was toast! The flames had risen up at a rate of knots and the dog's bowl full of water, which was all that we had, simply did not cut the mustard.

On her way back from a visit to one of her friends, the Queen of the whippy stick spotted the smoke, ran back, got a hosepipe and duly put the fire out. My friend was dispatched away back to his own home and then, in the blink of an eye, a lithe and lethal young branch had its life snuffed out as it was ripped boldly from the tree and blown to bits across the back of my legs (several times too)! So it was an early night for me minus my tea. Tough times but the Queen of the whippy stick calmed down after a while. (She also invested in a wooden spoon which she still has and which frightened me to this day.)

Anyway, hazelnuts and the run-down garage. I am getting there. Takes time.

Ever had a pet? We had a cat.

It snowed one winter and as usual I was up to no good in the garden. (Boy will be boys.)

However while looking for something to do I happened to look across to the farmer's field and saw a small black shape in the vastness of white. Ever keen for an adventure I locked my eyes firmly on my quarry and set off. Down through the garden, over the track that ran past the house, nip through the copse, hop the small stream and, hey presto, I was in the field. As I approached ever closer to my goal I could now make out that it was a small rabbit. Wicked!

It didn't move as I neared and stayed where it was as I bent down to stroke its cute little head. Poor thing must be freezing I thought so I picked it up wrapped it up in my coat and proceeded home.

I had a pet rabbit. When I get back I will tell my dad and we can build a hutch together. This will be great. My very own pet.

Upon my arrival I grabbed my dad and showed him my latest acquisition. With the utmost care my dad took the rabbit from me and with myself in tow we proceeded outside towards the old shed. In my eyes it would be only a matter of time before the hutch was ready.

Myxomatosis is not a word that regularly enters the conversation of a small boy and it is on that note that my dad produced a small and very sharp axe. The speed at which the rabbits head came off was something which required viewing with the aid of a time-lapse camera. Without so much as a word (and as THEY say) my dad 'Bagged it and binned it'.

A lifetime later, once the trauma and tears had abated, the whatnots and wherefores were explained.

Don't care don't care don't care. Robbie the rabbit was gone.

Siblings

Sisters or blisters
I really don't care
When you're young and you have some
They stink up the air

Sisters or blisters
They're one and the same
When you're trying to have fun
They ruin your games.

Sisters or blisters
Just get you down
You can't ever forget them
You can only frown

Sisters or blisters
If I had to choose
I think I'd have sisters
It's real funny when they lose.

Hey, I've got to tell you this before I continue. Living in the country, I did a lot of fishing and we ate a lot of game, and stiff like that. A couple of chaps used to call at the house on the odd occasion and sell my dad the odd animal that had been shot in the dead of night on someone's land.

Nothing wrong with that.

When I was a chef, I used to buy salmon at the back door that had net marks on the body. No questions, know what I mean.

Anyway, back to it and this is a real highlight.

The elder of my two sisters really is a sensitive soul. You know the score, hugs trees, saves the whale, cries when a plant dies. She is my sister and I lover her dearly, but there are times when she a lot in common with one of life's great foodstuffs. Fruitcake.

So to it then.

Blissfully aware of what was going on and under the belief - the fact is that my sister ate Watership Down chicken for years. Years I tell you!" When she finally found out, there were tears and, at one point, I thought that her had was going to pop off.

Oh how I laughed.

Onwards and upwards then.

Okay okay! I know. Hazelnuts. Here we go.

Back at the old shed then and it's a lovely summer's day. (Isn't that always the way. Just about every story you read, when something nice is taking place, it's always summer.)

For the purposes of what you are about to behold it really did all take place in the summer although for realism it should have been the darkest pit of hell. (This is actually case 1 now! Fancy that.)

So its a summer's day and there I was merrily shelling hazelnuts (YES!!!) with great gusto and a small rock when who should happen to pop up? Yes, you guessed it, the elder of my siblings. Interrupting what was by now a hive of industry did not go down too well and imagine the horror of it all when she tried to sneak a stray piece of nut from the two-brick high wall.

I have to tell you something and I promise faithfully that we will come back and finish this story but this is relevant and results in what must be the funniest thing that I have ever heard my dad say.

Needless to say I get on very well with my sisters now that we are older and on one occasion over Christmas and New Year Nicky and myself were visiting my parents. It just so happened that my sister and her son were also visiting.

As my mum's birthday falls on New Year's Day I had decided to cook and we were having roast pork with all the trimmings. I went all out to create a nice meal and served it up piping hot. The usual family conversation abounded throughout the meal and everyone commented on how nice it all was. Everyone except my sister. Meal finished and dad cleared away and then brought in the cake. We all sang happy birthday and my dad took what he termed as 'The same old photo' of my mum.

We all began to eat while my sister popped to the kitchen to get some cream I think it was. Not long after we became aware of a strange gagging noise. No one paid any attention for a bit but the noise got worse. Dad went out to see what was going on and promptly called my mum.

The sound had not abated so I wandered out as well. Lo an behold, there was my sister with a purple face and my dad handing out the Heimlich Manoeuvre! He was unfortunately not having much success so I calmly moved him away and had a bash myself. It took two good goes at it and finally a half chewed lump (more like half a pig) took a splat on the kitchen floor.

The sound of air rushing back into someone's lungs is a horrible one but with her lungs filled my sister promptly collapsed. I wasn't ready for that and nearly broke my goddamn back. Still I managed to stop her from hitting the deck and got her safely to a chair, sat back down at the table and carried on with my pudding.

How about that. She liked my food and I had just saved her life. Content I carried on munching.

Then in comes dad and in his quiet tone said …

'Well, that's what happens when you sneak off to snaffle pork.'

Fuck me, I laughed so much I nearly choked myself!!

Anyhow, there she was (Sorry we've jumped back about 30 years to the original story) trying to snaffle a rogue piece of hazelnut. It was such a shame then that she slipped (or was she pushed?) on some of the shells. One ear-piercing scream later and she was up crying and saying that her arm was broken. Myself not being the sort of chap that takes it all as fact (not since the lightening quick death of my rabbit anyway) told her in no uncertain terms that the arm was fine. I even took the time to wiggle it about for her to prove that it was ok. As luck would have it the arm wiggled in far more directions than was actually feasible so I ran and got my dad who took my sister to get her arm put in plaster.

That my friends was the crime.

Got to be frank with you now and, lads, pay real good attention. The female of the species forget nothing. Nothing. As soon as their memory banks are available for input in it all goes and will be stored for all time and is guaranteed to get you when the time is right.

Onwards and upwards then.

The hazelnut incident went away and my sister healed. (Good job too. The amount of wiggling she was lucky not to have a good arm and one that swings merrily in the breeze!)

Summertime then and the living was easy. Being that sometimes I could be a little bit mean to my sisters I took charge of my little sisters trike. We had a lovely steep slope in the garden that ran past the trees and, being far too big for such a small toy, shooting down at high speed was great. Using the toes of your shoes allowed the trike to come to a halt although wrecking my shoes would have its own forfeits.

Having gone down the slope several times I wandered off around the garden for a bit of a jolly. By the time that I had come back my sisters and their friends were playing on the grass. Obviously they would watch me on my death defying mission and then ask me for a go. No chance.

I began my approach and as I neared the start of my descent everybody was paying attention. Right then. Time to show off. Time for superspeed!

I fixed my gaze to my stopping point and went for it. I was a speed demon.

As luck would have it (again) I hadn't even got half way down when the rope appeared. Out of nowhere like one of those jumping mines.

My sisters and their friends had tied it to a tree and covered it over with some dirt. I kid you not and it caught me smack bang in the throat. Once again I was skillfully lifted from the saddle and dumped on the ground. The wind was knocked out of me and I lay there stunned. I vaguely recall my sister waving my arm in front of my face before they all ran away laughing.

And that was the punishment.

Moments later the sound of a trike hitting a wall rang through the air.

Whatʼs all this nonsense got to do with my parents then? Well, in a roundabout way its all about them. And parents in general. To put it simply you are your parents.

Have I lost you?

Look, it doesnʼt matter how much you rebel or how much of a shit you are in your lifetime, slowly you become like them. Exactly like them.

As I was reliably informed by my wife a few weeks back, I wash up the very same way that my mum does. I sound like my dad. I sit in the chair the same as my dad. I have the same outlook as my mum.

Get the point?

Good. We shall continue. There are many more crime files that are likely to thrust themselves in your direction but we can begin with a few facts of growing up that may be close to your heart.

Little boys get dirty. Its what they do and thatʼs a fact. On one occasion I had amused myself all day in the farmerʼs field and had, through no fault of my own, fallen in a cow pat (several to be fair). Upon my happy return home mum and dad noted that I was not only dirty but very smelly. I on the other hand was happy with my look and refused point blank to take a bath. Once again as luck would have it, it was now raining. My father grabbed hold of me removed my clothes and put me outside in the rain. My sisters of course found this to be hilarious. Hiding behind a shed I screamed at my dad and asked him what I was supposed to do. The kitchen door opened and shut. Seconds later a bar of soap landed nearby.

You see. Discipline in full effect. And I lose. Couldn't do that sort of thing in today's society but removing the plug from the gamecube works just as well. Another point of discipline now and one that is a hotbed of yes it did happen and no it didn't. I will always maintain that it did so here goes and sorry mum. (But yes you did!!!)

Playing with my friends near the mine, there is a spot where this grey stuff collects which is a sort of by-product from the copper. (I think.) It is slightly firm on top and if you move quick enough you will be ok. On this occasion no-one was moving quick. We were in fact taking turns to jump off the bank onto it! The whole thing was getting stickier and stickier and one lad had already lost a welly. I jumped and got firmly stuck.

I need to explain that it is not a question of get stuck pull your feet out an sod the wellys. No this stuff clamps on and holds you there in a vice-like grip. It also slowly begins to pull you down. By the time that it had reached my knees someone had decided that it might be a good idea to get my mum.

I was waist deep by the time mum arrived, heavily pregnant with my little sister and carrying a shovel. (Its not all in order you know!)

It took some time but I was finally dug out and received a smack across the backside with the blade of the shovel. Feeling very sorry for myself I was dragged off home for a bath. Discipline again and again I lose. But wait! Although I could regale you with all of the times that I was a little git it would get rather boring and you would see a pattern emerging so instead I will inform you of the only time that I actually won. Well and truly won! Sitting at the table for dinner I was shocked to see that sprouts were included in today's meal. Not for me. No way! No thank you. I progressed through my plateful of food avoiding the green balls from the land of Guff and when everyone had finished they still remained on my plate in all their glory.

Dad insisted that I ate one. As a small boy I gave him my best stuck out lip and look of sadness.

Didn't work and he still insisted that I ate one. After much stubbornness I eventually stuck one in my mouth but did not chew. I was reliably informed that I would not leave the table until I had eaten it. Well, that suited me. Three hours is a long time when you're little but that's how long it took.

The will of the parent was finally broken and my dad gave up. I spat the sprout back on the table and unfortunately got a clip for doing that. I had won though. Truly I had won.

It would be the only time.

Genetics

Our parents made us,
Not our world.
Genetic accident?
Force of nature?
Witness them then study ourselves.
One and the same,
Similar yet different.
They make us what we are,
Mould our future.
Without them we would not be,
Yet with them we are stifled.
The circle of evolution,
The road of destiny.
We too will soon join them,
Have children of our own.
The game will go on.

T ell you what. There's funny things that they do and there's bad things that they do. These things link up directly to things that you do in your own life.

Recently I got into making jams and things like that which my parents are big fans of. I also make sloe gin and have had quite a few rigorous attempts at wine. I manage to get it right because I remember.

I remember my dad making some beer in a dustbin. (A new one!!). It was one of those bins that have the clip-on lid. This I hasten to add was a first and last attempt at brewing up in those proportions. Mix made the top of the bin was secured as tightly as possible and was left in the dining room to ferment. I don't think my dad gave a single thought as to where the gasses would go and in the early hours of one morning there was heard an almighty bang which woke the entire house up. I do believe on that occasion dad was not popular with mum.

On the flip side of that, my most frightening memory was when for a little while mum was not popular with any of us!

Dad has always had a good job so it has never really been necessary for mum to go out to work. However in order to keep herself busy she, along with other mothers in the area, contributed to the local cottage industry by knitting hats and scarves from the local wool. These in turn would then be sold at a place called 'The Meeting of the Waters' which was frequented by tourists. She was of course paid for these but the sad part is that her children were her models. Some of the photos of us wearing those garments truly are hideous, but the hats and scarves themselves were very nice! My dad dressed me as a priest once and I myself have inflicted the same sort of torture and embarrassment on my own children although I did think that the leather jacket and bullet belt was a winner.

You may have noticed that mum does not feature that strongly but have no fear we have the pleasure of moving house in the near future and that's when dad takes a slight back seat.

I was asked once how come I knew so much about certain things and just about all of it was my dad, my dad, my dad.

I've already told you the cool stuff about the boxing but how about this.

As part of his job, dad did all the explosives at the mine. With the job came a VW pickup which to be honest I wish he still had as they are now collectors' items and worth a mint!

Explosives then. You could always tell when dad was off blasting because the armed police would turn up. It was Ireland in the seventies after all. They would all then trot off in convoy with my dad flanked on all sides to pick up the bang bang bars. I managed to go with him on occasion and in all honesty it was quite frightening to be surrounded by guns, but then again it went with the job.

I have also been allowed to wind the plunger up until the orange light came on and press the button. It fair made the ground shake I can tell you. Also even if you had not seen him go and had not heard the explosion , you knew there had been blasting as often there would be complaints due to the odd rogue rock (sometimes boulder) finding its was through someone's roof. These things happen though.

Its not long now before we can marvel at another crime and punishment scenario (bet you thought that I'd forgotten).

Before that though I'm going to take the time to tell you the sort of chap my dad is.

He reads books. He's got loads. At one time he was on two books a day. He is also the smartest and most hard-working man I know and it's sometimes a lot to live up to.

One time some boys lit a fire which got out of control and the men from the mine were called in to help the fire brigade. Dad kept going for two days solid. He only came home to grab a quick bite to eat and change his shirt. One time when he came back his shirt was still smoldering and he had not noticed that his back was burnt.

Another time he had heard whimpering and gone to investigate. Upon closer inspection he found that a dog had fallen down an old mineshaft. Dad being dad got some rope, went down and rescued it. A similar thing happened years later in Holland except that this time the dog was in a canal. In he went and got hold of the mutt and hung onto it until the arrival of the fire brigade to haul them both out.

See how it goes? These are some of the things that make a person great. In this case, my dad. These are the sort of things that it was necessary to live up to. This is what made him cool.

Quick crime fact time.

We always had a red car and it was always an Opel. The first one and second one for that matter were both Kadettes. Mark one was in the family for years and years. Good old RNI 884.

Shortly before the move to Holland dad bought a new one and not long after we had it we were once again out on a Sunday drive. Two motorbikes flashed by at speed and for some reason dad chose this event to see exactly how fast his new motor would go! There we were ragging it up the road in a desperate attempt to nip on the back tyres of the bikes. Dad with a glint in his eye, mum telling him to slow down, kids in the back seat loving it.

The police were only about half way through their doughnuts as both the bikes and dad passed through the speed trap in a blur. No fancy cameras then so it was bang on the brakes, sharp left turn and go like billy-o up the side road.

He had gotten away with speeding and because I have always assumed that my mum was magic, it seemed that from then on whenever we went out for a drive, it was her steely gaze that kept the speedo from going too high!

I got to drive trucks, diggers bulldozers and all sorts. I also got to go into the mine on several occasions. Now you tell me. Why is it that when two people (Dad and me) go into the same place, namely a side entrance to the mineshaft that one comes out looking the same as they went in and the other (me) comes out looking like the muddiest resident of the muddiest town in mud world? Answers on a postcard please.

Just to clarify. The aim is not just to heap glory on the exploits of parents or offspring but rather to allow you, the reader, to see that as you get on in life you remember more and more. You realise what it was that was done for you and how you have finally got to where you are. The biggest thing is who you have to thank for it. You may think that I'm talking shit here but really, take the time to sit and think on it. You may have worked hard in life and you may have paid your way. Like me maybe some of you have taken a long time before you started to pay your way. We all get there in the end but think not only about why you do things but how you do them.

Ah well, I'll leave that there for now as that is something that we can come back to.

To illustrate what I mean what follows are two poems. The first was written in 1990 when my head was in a really bad place and I was in the middle of a 10-year low. (More about that later.) The second was written in May 2005. From those I think you may get a glimpse of what I'm driving at. Crime and punishment will follow this I promise as we are in danger now of becoming serious and that, dear readers, will just not do!!

My father

He has always been a big man,
Strong for his family, for himself.
Success has not eluded him,
And the world is his oyster.

Many things of him I have asked,
Money mainly.
And he has gone without,
Pleasing one and all, no questions.

Through many times of trouble,
He stands by me always.
Forever finding some resource,
To keep me from falling.

Although I live in his shadow,
We are family one and all.
If I could go back and choose
He would always be the one.

I love him for what he is,
I know he will not change.
And if I ever end up like him,
At least I will have achieved something.

Summer 1990

Legend

The mans a goddamn legend
Worked hard all his life.
Bringing home the bacon,
For his family an his wife.

I know he's hard as nails
And I know he used to box.
But he's still as hard as ever
Even though he studies rocks.

He did his best to be there,
And we played a game of wits.
I did my best however,
To drive the old man tits.

I'm older now and wiser,
Dads one of my best buds.
I wish it had been like this before,
My life would have always been good.

I'd like to say I'm sorry,
For all the things I've done.
Sorry for being a rebel,
Sorry about the gun.

If I had my time over,
I think that I would see,
That I can be just like my dad,
Be all that I can be.

I love my dad to bits,
He really is my hero.
Without the help he's given me,
I'd be no more than a zero.

I hope he lives forever,
That mad dog dad of mine.
I hope he lives forever,
I wish we had more time.

My dads a goddamn legend.

Summer 2005

Mad Dog

So what would you do if you went on holiday with a couple of mates and left your kids in the care of some other mates? What would you do when you got back and discovered that all was not as it seemed? What would you do if you realised that there had been no control over the kids? What would you do as you looked round and realised that Lord of the Flies was not just a book? What would you do?

Read on, read further, read deeper and above all read faster. The following *true* story contains lack of respect, lies, violence, disbelief and, last but not least, attempted murder!

1974. Yes. The very same year that the two caricatures were drawn and the very same year mum and dad went on holiday with their friends to Norway. Dad's mate parked his car up at our house where it would be safe. Mum's friend, her husband and kids moved in. Mum's friend came because she was good with kids.

Don't worry it's all downhill from here!

With the folks gone the week started off well enough. Off to Dublin Zoo to look at the animals. Lots of sweets, a few e numbers, and then back home. Bit late when we got back so it was straight to bed after I had done a few monkey impressions. The following day was slow. It was all girls and me the only boy, so I amused myself. Dinner time was when it all began to take a tumble. The food was kak! And when I say that I mean the woman could not cook at all. If the cat had jumped up on the table and taken a dump on my plate I would have looked at it as a veritable feast. After that it was: Don't like the food. Get told off. Didn't listen. Get told off. Not going to bed. Get told off. Saying that you're not my mum and your food tastes like pooh didn't fly too well either.

Got told off.

Something had to be done and quick. A peace was called with my sisters and we held a pow wow. The woman had to go. But how?

As it turns out our kitchen was quite narrow but as luck would have it (and it really is lucky this time) it was lit up by a bulb of reasonable wattage. However this is not the lucky bit. No it was the fact that the bulb of reasonable wattage was sealed in by a very heavy looking glass lampshade. The plan was now afoot and this was to be our tool of 'getting rid of the kakky cooker!'

I stayed awake all night and in the early hours of the morning snuck down the stairs, very quietly got a chair and took it to the kitchen. Once there I unscrewed the lampshade and left it held in place by one thread only. One very quiet and theatrical snigger later the chair was back at the table and I was tucked up in bed.

Early morning saw us with cereal for breakfast (Thank God) and confirmation with my sisters that the job was done. We would now have to rely on lady luck to be on our side.

Can you see how devious little kids are? Don't be fooled. If they don't want to know and if they want you out of the way the same rule applies as much now as it did then. 'You're fucked'. No two ways about it.

Some of my friends had come round to play and all thoughts of ill will had· been pushed to one side.

When kids play isn't it amazing what they can forget even to go inside and use the toilet. I'm happy I'm playing who cares if I pee myself. 'Oops sorry I forgot' usually does the trick and then it's a slight scolding and a change of clothes so you can do it all over again. Try to remember that if you are a parent.

Back to playing and my sisters were in and out like yoyos. Girlies get the slightest bit of dirt on their hands and they just have to wash it off.

Out they came for the umpteenth time this time pursued by our nemesis who took great lengths to tell them that the house wasn't a stable that they could tramp in an out of at will.

This done woman who can't cook stomped back inside and slammed the door. As luck would have it (on a roll now) the good lady (good now because she is about to get it) reached the place where X marks the spot just in time for the lamp shade to release its grip and smack itself off her head. My Christ didn't she scream?! Knowing what had happened we all took a slow walk to see what had happened. There she was poleaxed on the kitchen floor.

To be fair the lampshade was still in one piece but in all honesty it really was a serious piece of glass. The same could not be said for the head of the downed one which flowed freely of the red stuff.

Her husband, being there at the time but alas not quick enough, reasoned that it was hospital time because stitches were needed (several as I recall). Into the car and off they sped.

This is southern Ireland don't forget. It was the seventies and we lived deep in the countryside so because nothing ever happened we were left on our own. Shall I repeat that. Six or more children home alone. Wouldn't happen today would it?

So, what were we to do? No parents and no thingy what's her face looking after us.

I know that this is a long one but everything happened on the same day. We knew that they had gone to Dublin hospital so it would be hours before they got back.

Wandering about, what took my eye? Dad's mate's car, that's what. It was a good old shape but to this day I do not recall what make it was. No matter. I had a good run at it straight onto the bonnet, onto the roof and slide down the back. Turn around, then straight onto the boot onto the roof and slide down the front.

Seen to be having a great time it was not long before I had been joined by the rest of the gang and great fun was had by all.

That's about the most interesting thing that took place that week. The lady in the bandages spent the rest of the week in a chair and her husband cooked (not bad either). The week ended, my mum and dad came back, the others left. That's it.

No? Ok then.

Well my parents came back at the weekend and words failed them. Close inspection and an insurance valuation later revealed dad's friend's car to be a complete write-off. Because so many children were involved no one really got told off. That's strike one.

Secondly, mum and dad apologised about the light and said that the thread must have weakened because the glass was so heavy. Mum and dad don't say too much but I know they were thinking, 'could've been worse, could've been one of us'. Apologies accepted they trotted off. Strike two.

We got presents. Strike three, perfect crime!

A shining example of times past and great days had all round. Although we had two small orchards at Dale House, we still went fruit picking on days out and dad found a great place where wild raspberries and, I think, strawberries grew. I tended to eat more than I collected. This again is something that I had learned about and would put into practice in later life.

When the first McDonald's came to Ireland, dad drove all the way to Dublin to get one and was gone ages because it was so busy. We had our cold Big Macs but that didn't matter; at least we had one. The milkshakes had been packed in dry ice. People had driven from all over to go there and fair play to the burger boys, they had invested in the dry ice so that people got their shakes home in A1 condition.

This was were I learnt about how they make smoke because dad put the ice in the sink poured on a little water and allowed it to melt. I will never forget that and thought it was magical.

I have in my time learnt a trick or two of my own that I have passed on to my children and I have a TV series called Due South to thank for that. The story is about a mountie and his exploits with his wolf. In one episode he picked up some dog pooh and stuck it on the end of his tongue. With that he knew the breed of dog, how old it was, where it had come from, and what it had last eaten.

Disgusted yet? Read on.

Where we live in Worcester there is a place called The Old Hills which forms part of the Malvern Hills but is on the other side so to speak.

It's the sort of place my dad would like. Full of fruit trees and little copses where on good days there are plenty of wild mushrooms to be had. There is plenty of space for the kids to run around and it is also educational for them. I and my wife take the time to show them stuff and they benefit in the long run. As is often the case when we are wondering around there is visible evidence of where the rabbits have been. Many is the time that I have selected a rabbit dropping and placed it on my tongue hereafter informing the children where it lives and even its name. (It would be nice if they were all called Robbie but he's dead. Cut down in his prime!) Nevertheless the kids think that it's great. My wife despairs and shakes her head.

Ireland was a funny old place but all the same it was safe and everybody was happy there. We lived in the middle of nowhere and were troubled by no one. It wasn't all acts of criminality and indeed much time was spent with my parents.

It would be good to try and go over everything that happened but then the danger is that it all becomes repetitive and then gets a bit boring.

Sure we played the sports teams and, yes, my sisters did their fair share of jigging about in the style of the Irish. The odd spat as you have read took place but it was never more than that.

As I have said before, my dad has always had a good job but, in his line of work, the rich vein of copper was not going to last forever.

Dad went away on a trip in late 1978. When he got back he was very happy and uttered the immortal line,

'How would you like to live in Holland?'

A close-knit family was about to hit a bump in the road.

We moved soon after.

Not a case of crime and punishment.

Just crime.

Off to the low country then but being as we must first fly over Blighty lets take a pit stop back at good old Port Isaac.

Because we went there so much it too forms a pivotal part of what shaped our particular lives. I had more of an affinity with the place than my sisters and after a while they stopped going.

So there it is, me on my own.

Do you know that just as I started writing this bit I remembered one more thing that I had to tell you.

One time in Port Isaac I was playing on the beach with my sister - scrabbling over the rocks and looking for small crabs and the like. It was also great fun collecting the pieces of glass that had been rounded off and frosted by the sea. You can find these on any beach you go to and if you collect enough of them, put them in a nice clear crystal vase with a tealight. Looks great. Just thought I'd tell you.

My sister had gone down by the breakwater and was amusing herself. What she had failed to notice however was that the tide had begun to turn and was on its way in. I had informed her not long before that it was nearly time to go for dinner. It wasn't long before the screaming started. Not because the water was now surrounding her and the rock she was stood on. No. It couldn't be that easy could it?

Apparently there was an octopus the size of a whale hovering around waiting to drag my sister off into the murky depths. Unable to convince her that an octopus had better things to do and she was seeing things I had no other choice but to wade in waist deep in water and rescue her. Back on dry land and unlike me not wet, no thank you - off she skipped telling me that we were now late and to hurry up.

Sometimes, in hindsight, I think that maybe it would have been better to have ignored the screams and walked back up the beach.

Slight interlude now before we continue. My dad's written three books now and the last time that we saw him he had nearly finished the fourth. Always knew that he would put pen to paper when he retired. Dad has kept a diary, or rather journal, of his life since at least 1963 and to this day takes the time in the evening to note down the day's events. If I had specific dates that I wanted to check up on then, with permission, that would be where I would look.

And so to the books. The first one was called *Skittery Grass* and was a collection of poems and phrases which he had grown up with during the war years and for a while after. I read it and laughed and smiled all the way through it. They were all things that my dad had told me when I was growing up and, in turn, I had told them to my children.

Here's my favourite.

Penny lament

I didn't come here to spit and cough,
I wanted to shit then bugger off.
Now here I sit, broken hearted.
I paid a penny and only farted.
A sad dilemma with which I wrassle,
I haven't got a three speed asshole.
If I had, one thing is clear,
I could have shit when in low gear.

© James Platt 2002

I never knew how easily and freely my dad could use the expletives of a four-letter variety.

The second book was a compilation of stories from north Cornwall, but the third book became a bit of a revelation. It was entitled *Your Reserves or Mine* and was a detailed account of his life as a geologist and all his travels. If I could get hold of some of the people that he has had to deal with they'd have a fucking good kicking and that's a mild as I can get where that's concerned. Then again I deserve one myself for a lot of the things that I have done in the past.

From the perspective of reading the book as an outsider, it is very interesting; but then for someone who knows the man, it is harrowing in places.

There are times in your life when you have a eureka moment. Not all of these are good.

I have a very good relationship with my parents but as you know it wasn't always like this.

My eureka moment happened as I read about dad working in south America. He had already become ill due to spending a lot of time at high altitude and the pressure of the job was very demanding.

In one passage of the book he had contemplated stepping out in front of a car to get a big enough knock just to get out of work. If he had not been married I think he would have gone.

At the time when all this was taking place, on the other side of the world was someone else adding to all the stress. Me. Bad time all round for myself but I had to put the book down as the tears were falling. I had not helped and all I could see was that I had also been responsible and pushed my dad towards that thought.

We have since spoken about it and I told him my thoughts. His reply was to say that it is all water under the bridge and we are where we are.

That's what makes parents parents and that's another reason for writing this. It all goes round and I expect that I will have my own share of dilemmas to deal with as my children get older.

Throughout everything though there has always been respect. That was the one thing that, no matter how bad it got, I always had. I still thank my mum for dinner and ask if it's ok to leave the table. I have never forgotten my manners and have instilled the same in my own children. It is a shame though that other parents cannot do the same. The youth of today are generally rude and on many occasions my wife has made me bite my tongue. I have had the pleasure of telling many people what it's polite to do whether they have liked it or not.

Please, thank you and eat properly at the table. Goes a long way and stands you in good stead for later life. Something else that I am grateful to my parents for.

It's all starting to make sense now isn't it?

Got to head back to Ireland quickly so that I can tell you the thing that I remembered to tell you but didn't and have now re remembered to tell you. You already know that the wood for the fire was kept stacked at the old shed. You know, the one with no roof and the two-brick high wall, scene of the alleged pushing incident.

That wood needed chopping and on occasion I would try to be helpful and do a bit. This normally occurred when I was in trouble for something or other and needed to score points big time.

Once I had erected a chickenwire fence around the vegetable garden while dad was at work. Did the trick that time anyway.

Chopping the way kids do involves taking a big swing and then belting whatever it was that needed belting. In this case the log. Things were going great until a big swing became just a little too big. I brought the axe back and bashed myself in the back of the head with it (short-handled axe.)

The wobbling ceased after a bit and I carried on but my head hurt like hell. Every now and again I would check it to make sure. I was working so hard and the sun was so hot that the paint on the handle had started to melt (red paint I hasten to add. Dad's favourite colour. Need I say more.)

I wiped the paint from my hands and cleaned the handle on my shirt. This operation carried on for a little while longer until, as luck would have it, I cleaned everything and checked my head before carrying on. Oh no, my head was leaking. Stunned, I dropped everything and ran screaming like a gibbon to my parents. Mum and dad both had a good look and decided that there was no need for stitches and therefore no need to go to the doctors. They would sort it out themselves and boy didn't they do just that. My head bashing move took place days before I was due to fly to England to spend the summer at Port Isaac. Remember this. Also please remember that I did mention that in one way or another your parents will get you back. Here presented on a silver platter was that very opportunity.

The solution to the bleeding head? Get a disposable razor and shave a bald patch on the back of my head. Then stuff a plaster on the cut. Thanks a fucking bunch. Any chance the hair is going to grow back in a couple of days? Yeah, one chance, sod all.

To add insult to injury I boarded the plane wearing my trainers, beige cords, t shirt and green (GREEN!!!!) sports jacket. Better still, the plasters had been removed so that I now resembled an apprentice monk with no dress sense whatsoever. I do remember mum and dad laughing while they told me that I could always wear a hat.

Off we fly then to the land of badly paid jobs, phantom octopus and roly smoking old men.

Jobs were always available especially in the summer and I worked every summer until I was 16. Thereafter until I left home I spent the next two summers working in Holland.

Port Isaac was the sort of place where apart from the level of expectation that was placed upon you there was also the petty jealousy and backbiting from the people who resented the fact that my parents were doing well for themselves. It was forced into me that I resented my mum for reasons that will become clear later on and the fact that dad was such a well-known local. There was the added bonus that everything that I did would be revealed and all that I did would bring shame on the family embarrassing my dad. I carried on regardless. Two things come to mind. One was just a run-of-the-mill thing and the other has since past into folklore, legend, have it how you will. It was great to be a teenager and have the power to impress your younger cousin. One time after going to the shops we got back to the house and I spun and kicked the gate shut. He thought this was great so being me and wanting to show off I opened the gate and said to watch carefully. One completed spin kick later and I had landed on the edge of a step and fallen.

The doctor told me that the plaster had to stay on for at least six weeks.

Undeterred I still managed to get about and with the aid of a stolen council ladder was able to get out of my room after bed time. Some bastard nicked the ladder back though and I was finally busted half way up the drainpipe struggling to get back into my bedroom! Upon arrival everyone told mum and dad that it had been a skateboarding accident. (Everyone in the family that is.) While talking to some of his old friends about this and that dad was informed that, 'he shouldn't have kicked the bloody gate.' So another ticking off came my way.

In the summertime loads of tourists passed through and plenty of people came to stay in the hotels. I had plenty of friends and we all used to go swimming in the sea at another place called Port Gaverne which was only over the other side of the headland and down the hill.

There is a place there known as Dead Man's Leap. It is a very narrow inlet and the cliff sides are not too far apart. Beneath the sea at the bottom are rocks seaweed and crabs. The idea is that if you watch the waves coming in and out it is possible to gauge when the time is right to jump. Not many people that I can think of in my lifetime have been stupid enough to go over Dead Man's Leap. Get it wrong and you're toast. Get it right and it's a bit of a hefty swim back to the beach or a long climb up the cliff.

You will be more than pleased to know that as a teenager I was that stupid and did indeed go over the edge.

As I jumped I panicked that I had gotten it slightly wrong. You see as the waves come into the gully the level of water rises but you have to jump before the wave hits the side end then you will get maximum depth. I missed it. Not by that much but a miss is a miss. It was indeed a very long swim round but I had survived although I had cut my leg and there were a few grazes on the side of my head. I have never asked my dad about Dead Man's, and he has never mentioned it.

I do know that he had swum from Port Isaac to Port Gaverne which is a hell of a swim. You need to be seriously fit to take that on and, as a boxer, my dad was. In truth the only reason I jumped was because as far as I was aware it was something that dad had not done and, in doing so, it had made me just as good as him.

Sad, isn't it, the length that someone will go to be like someone else. All my friends' parents knew my dad and had been friends with him so you're always up against it.

Sometimes it's the places that you love that help mould a person into what they are. There are times when I think that maybe I should never have gone there ever and there are times that I'm glad I did.

On the other side of that I did manage to have one thing in common with dad and that was sport - albeit a different sport. Whereas they would say that if he had carried on boxing, he would have been the best he chose to give it up. Should you go to a little village in Southern Ireland and speak to my hurling coach he would tell you, and to this day remains undeterred, that I was a natural talent and could have been the best. I never had the opportunity to find out about that though and, unlike my dad, did not give the sport up.

I had it taken away and that was yet another thing that made me angry. Very angry.

You wouldn't like me when I'm angry. Bet on it.

Beast of Burden

My anger dwells deep within me.
A great beast at rest.
Many have experienced its force.
Felt the intensity of the fire.
Once awakened it will not abate.
Once unleashed destruction is blind.
Control is hard but necessary,
The face of anger frightening,
For oneself and for others.
Step in its path,
And you will fall.
But the beast will sleep once again I know,
And will rise again I'm sure.
Stronger more direct.
Full of purpose and speed.
Removing all problems in its path.
No conscience, no remorse.
Then once again,
The beast will sleep.

Take a bag of frozen peas, remove one and chuck the rest on the floor. Study the one that you have in your hand, turn your back to the ones on the floor and throw your pea over your shoulder. Count to ten then turn round. Which one is yours? Can't tell? No problem, they all look the same they have no real identity to distinguish them.

That's what happens when you take a small boy from the country who has not yet had too many life experiences and place him in a city.

I love Holland and Holland loves me. My wife and I go there at least three, maybe four, times a year. If they're lucky we remember to take the kids. They also love it there.

In 1979 a family from Southern Ireland moved to Holland. Dad had a really good job with a metals company but it also involved a lot of travel. This placed mum in charge on basically a full-time basis. My mum is very slightly built and I refer to her these days as a wise old bird; but she is and has always been little and good.

We always had a packed lunch for school and a little change in our pockets to go to the tuck shop. Every day when we got home from school there would be a drink and something to eat which saw us through until dinner. I do sometimes feel sorry for single parents as, from my experiences in that country, that is what it must have been like for my mum.

We lived in a hotel at the very start while mum and dad found a house. The hotel was only a stone's throw from a massive beach and somewhere that we spent a lot of time playing on. It's been massively developed now but is still a very nice place to go to and take a walk. There was a drinks machine and an ice machine in the corridor and I had great fun running up and down getting ice and shaking the other machine until a can fell down.

Mum and dad had learned that they were building a new school outside the city and so we ended up with a house in that town. For the meantime though it was a case of a short train ride and then a bus to school.

Education is a wonderful and I instill in the children the value of paying attention in class and doing your best.

Education from my point of view, at least the type you get in schools, was a waste of time. I had no interest. Maybe it's because I had gone to a secondary school in Ireland for a couple of terms. It was run by priests and corporal punishment was still an accepted form of grabbing a child's attention. This in itself did not sit well and I thought that the priests could do with a hefty slap. Then again maybe it's because I had not had the opportunity to study French having lived in Ireland and when I got to school in Holland I was put back a year. That therefore made me the oldest and tallest in my class. No offence but I felt like a dick.

I did however take an active role in sports and my dad has plenty of 'I play rugby 'photos .

Nothing much of any consequence happened in the first couple of years. We all settled in and made friends. Dad did his travelling and life went on. It is then unfortunate that we all have to become teenagers.

Kids at school are mercenary bastards and when they feel that they have got someone on the ropes they are relentless in their pursuit. I never really had anything explained to me by mum and dad. They are not that kind of people. The ways of the world were something that you found out for yourself and, as far as they were concerned, the birds and the bees were nature's way of providing something to shit on you at any given moment in time. (How having a dirty great turd hit you from a great height is supposed to be lucky I will never know.) The other was something that would sting you if you pissed it off. There's a point there but I can't see it!

I may have been tall but at the time I was not big and therefore I stood in the firing line of the bullies. They did all sorts from pushing me around to calling me names. Some of the things I did not understand and it's sad when you have to go to your little sister and ask what indeed it is that they are talking about.

What she said I will never forget.

'Because you're coloured.'

Well! If ever a bombshell was to hit a child full on then that was it. Years before when I was playing hurling in Ireland I had been called banana man but I thought that it was because I had bendy legs! Sambo, jungle bunny and chimp boy were just a few of the things that I had to contend with on a daily basis but upon asking what I should do I was told simply to hit them. It was not as simple as that though. They were many and I was one. I did, as luck would have it (see, helps me all the time!) have a very nasty temper. On one particular day I lost it and punched a locked door. The force of the impact smashed the door off its hinges and straight to the back. It's a .funny thing, but that locker was the focus of attention for a while and the major bullying stopped. I guess they thought that it would be better not to be on the receiving end of something like that.

Little quips and things would carry on through life. A pile of drunken yobs shouted for me to get out of their country. I guess that ending their night bleeding was not the top of their agenda. I got a group of people together at school and we policed the bullies. My mum still gets thanked today for the help that saw her son safely through school. Since leaving I have bumped into one or two of the bullies who have come up and said 'Hello mate.' Like an elephant I do not forget and like a elephant they got stomped on. Oh, did I forget to say that I was now bigger and harder than they were now that school was over. No? Oh well. I had made it my mission to get them all in one way or another but my wife had managed to calm me down no end and, believe it or not, I can actually be reasonably logical and calm about everything. I will however not suffer fools gladly. Why is it that we cannot just all get along. Take the Forces for example. The army hate the navy and vice versa and they both hate the RAF. We're all on the same side. During my stint in the Royal Navy I discovered that sailors from Portsmouth did not like sailors from Plymouth. If there were ships from those ports berthed in a foreign port they were not allowed to be tied up together and special meetings were held with the ships company telling you what ship was in and what the penalties would be for fighting when we went ashore. Fancy that! While on the subject of fools, how annoying are those people who work as canvassers on the street. Can you give to this can you give to that, sign this and we will take your money, what catalogue do you use, do you smoke blah blah blah blah blah.

And the absolute worst of the worst are the god botherers. I know that we all have our beliefs but I have no wish to be out shopping with my family and be told that Jesus is watching. I really don't think he cares whether I abuse my credit card or not.

On one occasion we were visiting the potteries, an area around Stoke-on-Trent, and had been harassed no end by all sorts. Take this, do this, come to our pub, buy this. It was unfortunate then that while in not a very good mood the god botherer decided that I looked like the sort of person who could be spoken to. We did our best to slide on by but they were having none of it.

I would have tried to ignore it but the chap in question grabbed my arm to stop me from going anywhere.

'Hello brother', he said, 'stay a while, it's good news'.

If ever I did. How dare he grab me. Nicky knew exactly what was coming and to be fair to her left me to my own devices. This is a very good ploy on her part because if I can vent my spleen there and then I won't bitch about it for the rest of the day!

I rounded on the said member of the god squad and explained, 'Fuck you and your good news.' He seemed a little upset but we left him to ponder on that thought of the day They must have a network of people too because for some reason we were not approached for the rest of the day.

Now I'm not a racist and I do not see why people should be. I still get the odd comment at work but they do it in such a way as not to get the sack. A couple of the lads thought that I looked like Freddy Mercury and so I got the nickname of black freddy. Things like that I don't mind and can laugh off. Other things I do not like and therefore, in the same vein that they make comments in such a way to avoid being sacked, I tend to have a quiet word with them in the toilets which seems to do the trick.

As I said I am not a racist but on one occasion I had felt slightly like I was. One of my daughters is only four and is tiny. She is like a mini me of her mum Her friend is also no bigger than she is. It is my opinion therefore that if your child is being bullied at school and you find out about it then it is better to go to the parents rather than the teachers.

In the playground one morning Nicky found out that both our daughter and her friend were being bullied and having their snack taken away every day. We had had our suspicions but this confirmed it and my wife spoke to the mother straight away. They were English. The others were from Pakistan and would have to be handled differently. I could not see the parents and so would have to wait until after school.

When the kids came out I followed the child in question to her father's car and, surprise surprise, the whole family had somehow managed to squeeze themselves into the vehicle. I stuffed my head inside the car up to her dad's face and informed him in no uncertain terms that his child was bullying mine and that, as of this moment, the bullying stopped. He was also told that if there was one more incident, ever, then I would make it my mission to bully him for the rest of his life. I think that a couple of them wanted to get out of the car and have a go but four on one would not be a fair fight and it was a shame that I did not have any time to wait for a few carloads of their mates to turn up. As a passing comment I told them that if their child wanted to eat English food then they should pop to the shop and buy some.

Our daughter has been fine ever since. There is a whole book that I could write on the subject but I have no wish to be the subject of a death order. Funny as that would be my wife would not allow it.

The colour factor

Colour separates us all.
Black, white, yellow, red.
The four great distinctions,
Yet we are all one.

You see it on tv and in the street,
An old truth in a time forgot.
Other colours are seen as wrong.
Why then should white be right?

In the fight for a career,
It's experience that counts.
For despite your colour,
Nothing else should matter:

Will there ever come a day,
When we all stand side by side?
Can we live without,
The colour factor?

T here is an expression called 'you reap what you sow.' Dad sowed it, I bought it – and my parents both reaped the whirlwind.

In his travels dad always brought back presents. I happened to get the music. It has to be said that before the momentous moment where my life changed I had been given the soundtrack to 'Grease'. There was 'Super Trooper' by Abba and also a double cassette of the greatest hits of Elvis. On reflection it's all good stuff.

I was, however, a mod, or rather fancied myself as one. Had the trousers the shirts and the tie, even got close to buying a parka and sticking one of those RAF targets on the back. Didn't have the shoes though and that was a problem as neither myself nor my friends knew where to buy them. But wait. One of the lads had a brainwave that would not cost us very much money. And it was this.

We would go bowling.

So there we were in our very best clothes looking slick as ever wearing the crappiest shoes in our possession. We then proceeded to the bowling alley where we paid our small fee for one game. As luck would have it, we had to hand our shoes over and wear bowling shoes to protect the floors of the alleys. Red, white and blue they were. After a quick inspection of eachother and our feet, we legged it. The full ensemble complete. Having put enough distance between us and the man chasing us, we slowed to a walk and then a cocky strut.

We would listen to Smokey Robinson, Madness, the Merton Parkas, The Beat and, of course, The Jam. To be fair who wouldn't like The Jam? In all the years that have gone past, they are the only band from that phase of my life that I still listen to now and again.

However we must move swiftly to the life-altering moment and that happened when dad came back from a trip to America. He had stuff for us all and I was handed a brand new copy of 'Heavy Metal' the motion picture soundtrack. A double album and still sealed in plastic. I said 'thank you' as usual and wandered up to my room to play the record.

I wasn't expecting to be too impressed as the rest of my collection really was not anything to shout about. I put the first record on and lowered the needle. Bit of a crackle and the first track kicked in. Now when I say kicked in, my Christ didn't it just. Fair knocked me from my feet. 'The Mob Rules' by Black Sabbath. What a track. I was hooked. Rock music, heavy metal, call it what you will, had so much more to offer than anything else that I had ever heard. My friends changed as I explored the rock scene. I begged my parents for cash to go out and buy the latest albums by my new-found heroes. I was a rebel and I was living life large. I trashed my clothes, bought the badges and patches, had the bullet belt and wore the studs.

Every year in Holland they used to hold a free concert which was mainly for the unemployed. There were two stages and it went on for a couple of days. The

Bangles were playing and so too were The Boomtown Rats – but I was not heading to see them. This was to be my first ever live gig and the band in question was Tank. They had released an album called 'Filth Hounds of Hades' which, to my extreme joy, was rereleased on cd a year or so ago. I had already bought the album and it was solid gold.

All togged up, me and my mate made our way to the venue and were fortunate to get near the front. It was all open air and the weather was great. On the band came and our ears were assaulted for the best part of an hour. Fantastic. There were no other bands that we wanted to see so a quick drink later to cool down and we began to walk to the tram which was the first leg of our journey home.

In the early eighties in Holland there was a gang called the Greenjackets, and they were everywhere. I believe that they were attached to a football team or something. What I do know is that they wandered around in gangs and it was very seldom that you found one on their own.

One thing though that they had in common with mods was that they hated rockers and we were being followed.

This was not a pleasant position to be in. We had just been to a great gig and were now about to get japped. My friend was very nervous. Well that's a lie: he was shitting himself. As was I. We could see the tram in the distance and I told him that, as soon as we rounded the corner, to run. Once again, as luck would have it, he ran before we got to the corner. Fucker! The chase was well and truly on. I caught him and passed at a gallop. No way I'm bleeding today, It really was touch and go but we made it to the tram. They were banging on the tram as it pulled away, but we were free to run another day.

Even at school there were many run-ins with the Greenjackets. They did not like the posh English kids in their school uniforms wandering around their town. Funnily enough, years later I bumped into one that I used to square up to on a regular basis and we got on like a house on fire. Just goes to show how age can change a person.

On one occasion at a rugby tournament some of the juniors picked on some baby Greenjackets and thereafter arranged a fight. It was to take place at the local train station. A good piece of advice now is never trust the people who think that they are hard and can take on the world. Trust those that will watch your back in a tight spot. As it turned out, there were not too many of them and only a handful of us turned up. Now, when you are a teenage boy who thinks that they rule the world with mates who think the same, here is something to bring you back down to earth with a serious bang.

The Greenjackets were very well organised. With the arrival of the train, a bus turned up followed by cars, motorbikes, bicycles, and some on foot.

Everything, and I mean everything, contained Greenjackets. They appeared like ants swarming from their nest to defend their patch. There were only six of us. Standing your ground results in a smack in the mouth and there is no way to fight back unless you wanted to become a stain on the ground. We were marched to a platform and pushed on a train out of town. Out of town! we lived in that town. And we had no money. And we had to walk home. And it rained. Rock and bloody roll!

I went to several other concerts after that: Judas Priest, Ted Nugent, Raven, Maiden, Thunder, Highway Chile, The Screaming Jets. You get the picture. By far and away the best band I ever saw when growing up was Motorhead. Good old Lemmy in full effect. There were all sorts there. Rockers, skins, punks. Young and old. Over 2000 people crammed into a space for 1500. Fantastic. I stuck my head in one of the cabinet speakers. Couldn't hear for a week. Bloody brilliant.

In recent years I have not been so outgoing and have only been to pubs really to see tribute bands but some of them are really good. I managed to see Saxon at a nightclub when I was a student and they were on a comeback tour and not so long ago I took my eldest daughter to see The Rasmus. She had been to one of the local radio festivals with the Mickey Mouse bands but this was her first ever rock concert. Being me, we got there early had something to eat. When we went in I managed to get to the front. A great time was had and after wards I bought her a t-shirt and poster from the touts outside. Unfortunately now that she is imminently to become a teenager the rock has fallen by the wayside and the style of dress is townie – whatever that is – and the type of music is rap, hip hop and RnB.

I still play my music as high a volume as my wife will allow and my rock roots are firmly in place. The music has changed somewhat from what I started out listening to. Nu-metal, speed metal, death metal, thrash metal, melodic rock, AOR and stuff of that ilk. The band of the moment is Trivium. My wife hates them and the kids are not sure. Because the lead singer screams for most of it before he sings properly, my youngest daughter whom I have converted into a proper rocker has naturally assumed that he was practising first before he played properly.

She is now this way, much to the despair of her mum, because they bought me the DVD of all of Iron Maiden's videos. Eddie is now one of her heroes and she is determined to marry Blaze Bailey.

This of course is all my fault. Five-year-old girls shouldn't really be watching a skinless zombie chase the devil around the stage while five men with long hair sweat to the beat.

Can you see how it goes? Yet again the pattern emerges and we come full circle. I have loved that music for over 24 years now: I am simply sharing it with my children.

You reap what you sow and rock till you drop.

Thanks dad.

You will be pleased to know that the leather jacket, complete with patches, studs and badges is still intact. The music is louder than ever and you are never too old to rock and roll.

Hard Times

There is a slight downside to being a hard rocker. With that comes the responsibility of being a hard drinker!! And to be fair I gave it a damn good go.

When I was growing up in the eighties in Holland it was legal at 14 years old, yes 14, to go into a bar and buy a drink. How cool was that?! Now that I am older, however, it does not seem like a good idea and I would not like my children to be boozing at that age. Once again you see that you are turning into your parents.

Bad things happen to people who abuse alcohol. One time in Port Isaac, I had been to the Hunters, which is a bar/hotel at the top of the hill. Back Hill or Rose Hill I think that it was called. Now, when I say that this hill was steep, I mean steep. Take a sheer cliff, lean it back a few degrees then make it slippy. Add to that a few bends and make it really narrow and there you go.

On this particular evening I had gone a step too far and had consumed more than was necessary. While stumbling back with my friends (well if they really had been my friends they would not have let me do it, drunk or not!) another so-called friend pulled up on his motorbike. This to me looked like an interesting thing to do. So I grabbed the helmet from his hand and thrust it on my head as best I could. I think there was a slight debate on his part on whether I should be doing this but it fell on deaf ears. It may also be of note that this particular bike had been modified. None of your modern day 'all the power is there from the start'. No, I should be so lucky. This was the time that when you reached a certain level of revs the full power kicked in, and it was a case of hold on tight.

So I had the bike and took it for a spin. Once down the hill was great; back up and down for a second bite of the cherry. Hammering down, blind drunk in the dark with no lights on. Powerband at full scream. Fortunately the state that I was in meant that there was no hope of using the brakes to any great effect and as the road ran directly onto the beach I was in danger of entering the sea and making an underwater attempt to reach Ireland. Not a bad idea come to think of it.

Anyway fortunately.

Fortunately there were a pair of concrete steps sticking out into the road attached to one of the hotels. Best braking system I have ever come across. I hit them almost full on at a stupid speed (I think) which in turn enabled me to remove the helmet without touching it and also allowed me to roll and slide for about 50 yards or so. In all honesty I should have been in a bad way or, worse, dead. My only saving grace was that I was drunk – which I know to be a contradiction in terms but there you have it.

I do not really drink anymore. The odd glass of the sloe gin that me and my wife make and the odd single malt with a cigar if the mood takes me. Oh, and I mustn't forget that after lengthy debate with my youngest daughter, when he comes to our house, Rudolph gets the usual carrot and Santa – because he is cold and stressed out with all the houses to visit – gets to chill out in our house for a few minutes with a large glass of 12-year-old Isle of Jura single malt, a homemade mince pie and a King Edward cigar. And there is always a note in the morning saying 'thank you'.

So the drinking started when I was around 14 years old. On a Friday after school dad, if he was around, would give me 25 guilders. This was then pocket money. That money allowed me to get a return ticket on the train, buy my cigarettes for the night. Forgot to mention that ever since being cornered in Port Isaac at the age of around 12 and forced to puff on a cigarette I had taken up the habit.

The rest of the money went on booze and there was enough left over at the end of the night for a burger on the way home. I can't really remember if I was ever given a curfew but mum and dad knew that the last train left at about 12.45am.

There were two pubs that all the British kids went to. One was called Queens and the other was simply known as The Oranjeboom. It was unfortunate that before I left Holland my sisters were both old enough to frequent these places with their friends, so what street cred some of us had kind of went out the window when our siblings turned up.

So the plan was a simple one. Happy hour at Queens ran from 5.30 to 6.30 and happy hour at the Oranjeboom ran from 7 until 8. We would leg it home from school, get ready, then all meet up at the station. Buy our ciggies at the main station when we got there and take a slow amble to our first destination.

Not to put too fine a point on it, happy hour means that for the hour you get your drinks half price. This was Holland and the rules did not seem to apply there. Happy hour meant buy one get one free. And these were not pints. The Dutch served very strong beer and in half litres. Pay your money and get two glasses at one go. One litre of beer! 14 years old and I'm holding a litre of beer in my hands and I can go and get some more. It was drink that and do your best to stagger to the next pub for another hour of blind stupidity. It did not take us long however to get a grip on the situation and start drinking sensibly. As sensibly as an evening of strong beer would allow you to.

Between both the British pubs stood the pub where all the American school drank. Not only did we enjoy beating them at rugby every time but on our way from one pub to the other we would indeed give up some of our valuable time to clip a couple of them. This was usually just for something to do, but that again, dear readers, is a whole other story.

That was mainly it and what formed the pattern of our lives. School and drink. Many was the time as we got older that we would nip off from school at lunch and go to the chippy or local pub for a ,brew and then back for afternoon lessons.

And so we now begin to approach dodgy ground. My dad was always away and therefore my mum was in charge. My temper had become worse and when he got back from his trips my dad could no longer exercise any control over me. Many a time, small as she is, my mum has stepped between us as the shouting started and we began to square up. It had reached a decisive point that it had indeed been a mistake, especially on my part to move to Holland. Any closeness that I had shared with my parents was almost gone. I would listen to my mum and sometimes talk with her about a great many things; but with my father and sometimes my sisters I could not stand being in the same room. It got so bad once that it began to affect my parents marriage, and they almost reached a decision that in order to keep the peace it would be necessary for me to move out.

These are things that I do not want to write about and there are other parts that I wish to skip altogether. After lengthy discussion with my wife it was decided that some things need to be included because otherwise it will not all fit together. Some of the choicer words that I use do not sit well with her but they come across on these pages exactly how I speak.

There is nothing that she does not know about my life but there are things that my parents do not know. Nicky does not want to read them, I do not want to write them but you would not see the real me if I did not. My life has been full and I have lived it to the very edge. There was a time when there was nothing that I would not do and nothing that I would not try.

Sometimes I will ask my wife why people do the things they do and sometimes I will cry about it. One time although my kids see me for me the youngest one came home and said that I was blackie/brown. It was funny at the time, but what is it that makes people tell children these things?

I may not have taken the time to take advantage of the school education that was being given to me but I made damn sure that I had a streetwise life education. I have gone from being what I was to being a father myself and although I have not been perfect my lifestyle has allowed me to be in the position to be able to advise the children on the pitfalls. I am able in general to recognise problems as they occur and remedy the situation. I went my own way. I fell. I got up and I came back from the edge. So, no, my mum and dad did not prepare me in any way for the type of life and country that I was being thrust into. There was a time when I was very bitter. Angry that I had not been told. Resentful that I was unprepared. I am older and I honestly honestly owe them a debt of thanks. They did push me in the direction that shaped my life but because I made those mistakes I had to learn to adapt and survive. Today's world is a dangerous one and those that enter it need to be prepared. They need to survive and unfortunately they will not get the life skills that they need at school. My children will get theirs from me.

Just by being themselves my mum and dad have allowed me to be in the position to protect my kids and once again I thank them.

I have no worries.
My children will leave and enter the big wide world.
I have no worries.
My children will survive.

Once is enough

I've tried it a couple of times.
Drugs that is.
I really liked it.
I don't do it all the time.
Take it or leave it, that's me.
I need to get some more though.
Addicted?
Not me.
It's just something to do.
I'll stop one day.

In Holland there is only so much beer that you can drink before you get bored. There are only so many tulips that you can look at. There are only so many chips that you can eat with mayonnaise.

Bored, bored bored bored.

If you look hard enough and have the right sort of information, as they say in 'Star Wars', there is always a path to the dark side.

In my life I have chased the dragon, skinned up and smoked the fatboy and if I had been a skier then my favourite type of snow would have been the fine white powder.

Cannabis was legal in Holland. The other drugs were not. Because of this, unlike other countries, it was something that we were well informed about and something that we did just because it was there.

I helped my friend make a space cake once and we ate it all. No effect so we both felt a little disappointed. Didn't realise that you have to wait for the food to start digesting before anything happened. While cycling home I had a big hit all of a sudden and passed out. Woke up next to a canal covered in dog poo.

This is not a subject that I wish to dwell on and suffice to say that once I had started then the change was evident and can even be seen in photographs. My dad suspected and my mum knew.

I came in one night and she sat me down and asked me to show her what I was smoking. I tried to deny it but it was to no avail. So we discussed it. What it did. How much it cost, stuff like that. When the conversation was over my mum told me that if I carried on then I was to leave the house and her and dad would never help me again. Once my mum set: herself on a course of action then that's that.

Needless to say it was a miracle cure and I left it all well alone. I was to have more than enough on my plate later on.

Maria

I have always been superstitious you know. Everything happens for a reason, wave at magpies. That sort of thing.

I think that my mum has loads of magical powers. She used to do tarot cards but stopped when she saw some bad stuff.

She knows stuff about stuff and can talk on every subject that you can think of. If you were ill my mum could cure you with a wink and a blink. Failing that there are always the obscure remedies.

There was a time in South America when I had such a cure!

My good old dad bought some cream cakes. I firmly believe that he left mine on the window ledge to warm in the sun and then chilled it again before I got to eat it. Can't swear to it but how do you explain why within a matter of hours why I was the only one running to the toilet with the trots. Got to be a conspiracy there! The cure in this case? Chug down on a lump of coal. That's the cure. Apparently, like milk, the coal lines your stomach and in turn binds you up. Not the most logical of explanations I know, but it works so who am I to argue?

Now one time I was very ill whilst living in Chile. The cure for that was what I referred to earlier as one of my mother's witches brews. This is not something for the faint-hearted.

Witch's brew I

Cinnamon stick
Bayleaf
Eucalyptus leaves
Honey
Spices
Lemon Juice
Boiling Water

1. Take a spoonful of honey and drop it in a large mug.

2. Shred rip and squeeze the remaining dry ingredients and place them in that same mug.

3. Squeeze in a good whack of lemon juice so that the sweetness of the honey is overpowered.

4. Pour on the boiling water and allow the whole lot to infuse for a few minutes.

5. Stir and take the spoon out. Remember *not* to remove the bits that are floating about.

6. Make your intended victim drink it all up with no excuses.

7. Laugh as they struggle to keep it down while swallowing.

8. Check the cup when they have finished and then hand it back saying that there is still a bit left.

Witch's brew II

Chilli sauce
Sugar
Ground ginger
Whisky
Hot water.

No method for what to do with this one. Simply stick it all in a cup and give it a stir.

Hand it to the intended victim and, as they drink, put your hands on your hips and laugh like a maniac as the victim's face contorts and turns green. Walk away continuing to laugh as long as breath allows!

My mum's gonna smack me one for this ...

You know that, don't you?

Funnily enough it works and in a matter of hours you will feel right as rain.

Good old mum!

Descent

Beg for it
Borrow it
Steal it
Kill it
Get it
Roll it
Smoke it
Drink it
Sucked into it
Immersed in it
Kicked out of it
Get over it.

T he pattern had emerged. My dad was never around – which was not his fault – my mum was doing her best but my head was long gone.

I was doing my own thing and hell bent on a path of self destruction. Consequently the exam results which I achieved speak for themselves. Not much, no how, no way.

All things being equal though I still had my dad. He took the time to phone around and got me a place at Plymouth College of Further Education. I was to train as a chef.

First things first. Apart from going to Port Isaac I had no affinity with England so my request to take a year out fell on deaf ears. It was where I was meant to live and that was that.

Secondly, and make no mistake and with the greatest of respect, mum and dad wanted me gone.

But hey, thinking of gone, that reminds me.

One time when we were little and on one of our trips to Port Isaac we went on a day trip to Exeter I think it was, but then again it could have been Plymouth. No matter, it was a trip out. The shopping was boring, as was everything else, and in particular my sister was irritating me no end. I had a plan.

I knew that we would be going back to a certain shop and so bided my time. Once there we slowly moved closer and closer to my goal. After what seemed like an eternity there it was – the lift. Attention was not on us as the day-trippers were only concerned with buying as much as possible in the time allowed. The doors opened and in I stepped, whereupon I called my sister to join me. As the doors were closing I jumped out. Mission success. One sibling down, one to go.

Some bad things happened after that. Upon being asked where my sister was I got a clip. Then we had to use up valuable shopping time to go and look for her. Worse still. We found her. I got a clip. Once the story had been relayed? Yep, I got a clip.

And so off I was shipped to enter the big wide world and look after myself. I lived in a bed and breakfast for a little bit, which dad paid for, and I had an allowance of £25 a week which came in the form of a Dutch giro cheque.

The amount was never filled in to begin with and being the shitty person that I was I would alter it so that I could cash it for more. Thinking back I regret it all but at the time – well actions speak louder than words. Nothing was ever said and eventually the cheques came properly written. Not long after they stopped.

During my time at college which I found to be quite easy (I had a flair for cooking believe it or not), I drifted in and out of several bedsits and had to do some part-time work in order just to get by.

There was other part-time work that I had but I have no wish to go into any type of detail as some of the files may still be open …

Just read the next page.

Stealing home

You're in,
Heart pounding.
Thump, thump, thump.
Ever nearer,
Moving toward your goal.
A distant siren.
Freeze.
No movement.
No sound.
Heart pounding.
Thump, thump, thump.
Sweat falling.
Closer still.
Case.
Glass cuts.
Delicate.
Turn.
Quickly leave.
Heart pounding.
Thump, thump, thump.
Edge away.
High jump.
Observe.
Wait.
Moments pass.
Running.
Heart pounding.
Thump, thump, thump.

Y ou may have noticed that the pace has picked up a bit and we are at present moving swiftly along. There are many reasons for this and most of them are summed up in the sheaf of poems that will appear in a bit.

1985 - when I first moved to England - up until the summer of 2002 are years that are best forgotten and in short not written about.

17 years that I simply wish to burn from my mind. There were a few great things that happened but until 2002 the general frame of mind and spirit did not change.

Wanna know why? I'll tell you. I, me that is, was a damn good chef. There is no need to blow my own trumpet, the facts speak for themselves. Both my wife and my mum tell me constantly that I need to write a cookery book. Maybe after this one. Who knows?

I worked in this profession until 1999. A year after leaving college I was a head chef but soon realised that I had way loads to learn and so got a different job at the bottom of the ladder. It took me a couple of years to build myself back up and it wasn't long before I was top dog again. This rise however coincided with the departure of my parents to further fields. They did in fact get transferred to Chile in South America. A body blow in itself - I felt that I had even less places to turn to and even less people to talk to. Bouts of depression would lead to self harm and I even stabbed myself in the side of the head near my eye just to get some attention. Years later I had lacerated my arms through stupidity.

However, with my parents gone and not much else to look forward, I spoke to no one and made the decision to end it all. I was a head chef at the time and during my break after the lunchtime rush I went to the local chemist. I told them that I was going on an expedition and suffered from headaches. They gave me 250 strong paracetemol. I went back to the restaurant as there was work to do. I was on my own in the afternoon and while making desserts for the evening, started taking the tablets. I was told later that I had eaten 196 of them. I had felt tearful while doing it but could really see no other way to solve my problems. By the time that I had become woozy I had begun to regret the decision to take my own life and staggered to a local shop. I told them what I had done and they called an ambulance. I remember being given something to make me sick and I remember the sound of the sirens. I know that my stomach had been pumped because the nurse told me that I had torn the tube out of my throat and ripped all the lining. I woke up attached to many tubes and a lot of bleeping. I had been in a coma for three days. They had struggled to stop my liver from collapsing. I had only just survived but it was touch and go. I survived with even less. I had no visits in hospital. I had no calls. My parents did not know. When I was finally strong enough to leave hospital I discharged myself and, because I had no money, walked the 15 miles home.

I lost my job and my place to live. There was nothing. No funds. No fun. No future. A few more uninspiring weeks later, and a little more trouble, I went to Holland (long story …) and stayed there for a couple of weeks as a homeless vagrant. Begging for food and stealing. Just to get by. Someone did help me and I made it back to England. I went to Port Isaac. Within a month I had self harmed badly and they tried to put me in a mental institution.

Not long after I was sent a ticket to fly out and see mum and dad. I would get better, and in all those times of trouble there was to be one of the greatest times of my life.

Top of the World

Father and Son

Blood rush

Trapped in a void that is forever mine.
My blood pulsating through me.
Forever faster and with more power.
My life force forever with me.

I've drained this force more than once,
And seen the system at work.
How I marvelled at the sight.
The ingenuity of its design.

The day will come when all will cease,
My veins will lie still and hard.
Never to rush, never to pump.
Forever still.

Once depressed

Once depressed
Sleep comes where you can find it.
Stuck in ever decreasing circles.
Unable to rest.

There comes support from many,
Sharing their hopes for you.
But with nothing to begin with,
How can one be happy.

Everything seems so pointless,
But you dream of rising up.
To face the world full on.
To free that growing stress.

See

Seeing faces smiling round you,
In a world that is so cold,
Makes you stand up and be happy,
Instead of feeling blue.

It's not very hard to do your best,
To stand up and be counted.
The difficulty is convincing yourself.
Once depressed.

Strong and silent

I sit here now in my padded cell,
Rocking forever rocking.
How long I have been here I do not know.
How long I will stay not certain.

Four walls all covered in foam,
The floor, soft to the touch.
Lights as bright as the sun,
A camera in every corner.

And watch they do to see my moods.
They say I'm completely insane.
Mad as a hatter and all that jazz,
But only I know the truth.

One day they shall release me,
Swap this jacket for another.
A return to reality in their eyes,
But what is real?

My mind is still a blur,
What I did I do not know.
This padded cell my home forever.
My sanctuary.

I speak no longer,
For words are hard to form.
So here I sit in my padded cell.
Rocking, forever rocking.

Cooking's all bullshit you know.

One place where I worked you take the leftover gravy from lunchtime, add a load of fried onions and a couple of bottles of red wine put some in a bowl and stick a cheesy crouton on top. Hey presto! French onion soup, £3.50 a pop.

Some odds and ends of fish that are hanging about. A few leftover prawns. Lob it all in a dish and cover with a bit of white sauce cheese and herbs. Top the whole lot off with mashed potato and bake in the oven. What you then have is 'a medley of fresh local fish bound together with a rich cheese and herb sauce topped with pureed potato'. Served with vegetables of the day, £8.50.

And it's all bloody bollocks.

This was not the type of cooking but it is an illustration of the way in which artistic license is used to tuck up the punter with absolute crap. They all do it. A chef's favourite ingredient is demi-glace. Thick gravy to the likes of you and me. With that you can make any sauce known to man and charge the earth for it. Bear that in mind the next time you're out for a meal and the sauce is extra.

My cooking won me awards and took me places. I was a head chef in many fine hotels, had the AA Rosette awards for excellence and was not far from the coveted Michelin star. My signature dish was a soft meringue roulade served with forest fruits and a drizzle of red wine and cinnamon coulis. I won a prize for that one.

I had some regular customers at one place and they took me to the West Indies to work for them. I had a wealth of experience and still do. The hours are a killer though and so are the shifts. I want to be able to enjoy my life and the children and have quality time with my wife. Therefore it has all now gone. Cooking at home is enough, and for my mum and dad. As you read earlier, my food is so good it fair chokes my sister up!

Tell you what though. Want to know what the single greatest thing I have ever cooked in my life is?

You do?

Good good good.

But first a bit more of a ramble.

Having flown out to Chile I learnt Spanish and my parents made sure that I saw the dentist and had my teeth sorted out. Also saw a psycho doctor, but he hadn't got a clue either.

I went up one of the landmarks with my dad called Cerro de san Cristobal, which is St. Christophers Hill and actually stood where the Pope (God rest his soul) had given a sermon. I met quite a few genuine people and a lot of shysters - but I had been forewarned about them.

One day dad asked me if I would like to go up to the mountain camp with him. Must explain that dad was in the mountains for two weeks and back down for a week. How he did this for nearly 10 years I will never know.

His nerves were shot from the constant altitude changes and it was a humbling experience to see the man, my big dad, hesitate to cross the road. This was the man who took me rock climbing without ropes.

One time I remember that dad showed me which bus to catch so that I could get to the mountains. I said goodbye and got on. As the bus left someone was tugging on my sleeve as I attempted to get to the back of the bus. I shrugged it off but the tugging continued. Being of short temper I spun round to smack the person but it was dad. He had nearly been caned by another bus as he waved me off and had no choice but to jump on this one! He did not have the right change and was tugging to get my attention!

And so back to the mountain camp. This involved flights to several destination and then a shortish flight in a very small plane up to the mountains. The plane lands on a sort of plateau and the airport is no more than a garden shed. It is then a short drive from there to the camp.

We were at about 450m above sea level and I was given strict instructions about Puna. Altitude sickness.

Take off

Strapped in door shut.
No way out.
Moving slowly.
Nervous sweat.
Small window.
Nothing to see.
Still moving.
Turning always turning.
All stop.
Passengers silent.
Engines roar.
Movement begins.
Speed increases.
G force.
Praying.
Nose up tail down.
Airborne.
Stomach drops.
Climbing climbing.
Level out.
Relax.

Altitude

Higher than you've ever been.
Air clean.
Crisp.
Sun beating from blue skies.
Walking slow.
Breathing hard.
Among the clouds.
At one with creation.
No buildings.
No cars.
Vast expanse.
Eerily silent.
Peace.
Top of the world.

You won't get very far if you break the rules. I had two. Don't try and do too much, and if you find yourself in a whiteout stay where you are until it clears. Many a person has fallen off a mountain through being clever.

Dad had a cabin all to himself and that was where I was staying. There was plenty of oxygen on tap if need be and there were times in that week that I was very grateful for the supply.

Dad took the time to show me around and we went down the mine shaft so I could see what it was that he did. Altitude sickness got me slightly and the chef there boiled up some weird looking flowers and made me drink it. This helped somewhat and I was also taken down 2000m so that I would find it easier to acclimatise. I met some of the indigenous people and they sold me a beer at a very inflated price! But they were very nice and told me about the area and some of the animals and food that grew there. Dad took me across the border to Bolivia where we could see the highest mine in the world. Only Bolivians could hack that and it didn't look that much higher than where we were. I also crossed into Peru where we were able to see the sulphur train fully loaded and ready to go.

At one time we had the misfortune of getting the truck stuck and were unable to shift it and so had a very long walk to make. I found it hard going and had to stop. Dad carried on and brought me back some water in his helmet and helped me the rest of the way. The air is very thin up there and, if I remember correctly, removing his helmet for my benefit had allowed the sun to burn his face. I was grateful and ashamed at the same time.

The food wasn't too bad and sometimes it seemed that dad had to make the best of a bad deal. One of the staple things on the menu were empanadas. These are little parcels filled with meat but because they use so many herbs when you bite into one the contents have turned green!

As a favour to him, dad asked if I could show the chef there how to make Cornish pasties and that, my friends, is the greatest thing that I have ever had the pleasure to cook. Cornish pasties for my dad. I can't say if they were any good but dad enjoyed them very much. I had had a great week and it was a shame that I had to leave. There were tears and I thanked my dad. The time we had spent was reminiscent of Ireland and it was something that I miss very much.

Not long after that I left and went back to England where I carried on as best as I could. I would go to Chile again but not to the mountain, nor the camp. That was a memory best treasured.

By the mid nineties mum and dad moved back to Holland and it was then possible to go and see them often.

My children, all seven of the little buggers were born in the nineties and although I had some bad times I would not change them for the world.

There was only one other highlight in the nineties that would in later years change my life and alter it beyond recognition.

In 1996 I met my wife.

**Super Stern
and his wonderful ever-patient wife Nicky**

Let me explain

There are trends in life that we all follow. Be it the food we eat or the clothes that we wear. The car that we drive or the type of things that we buy for the house. Everybody is a victim.

Body art is my trend. Tattoos. Skulls, dragons and flames on one side. Flowers birds and flames on the other. Everybody has a good and a bad side. My wife's name is on my back. Designed by me. It sits in pride of place and will not be joined by another. They hurt. Fact. Sometimes you enjoy the pain. Sometimes you feel that you deserve the pain. You get addicted to it for a while. Other times you become needle shy. They cost. To date on my skin in excess of £3000. But mine are original. Hand drawn and the design binned after. It began as a fad. People say that it was to cover up my own colour. Wrong. Wrong. Wrong.

In the summer as my skin darkens the scars stay white. They stand out. I have to explain. I became sick of explaining There are too many. Now no one notices. That is reason one. The other?

I like them and they are now a part of me. I am not ashamed.

They do not make me a bad person. I have not turned into a thug.

They are the same as my personality. Colourful.

Just thought that you should know that.

I have loved my wife from the very first day that we met. The first time that I saw her I thought to myself, 'Why can't I have one of those.'

Tall, blonde, stunning. Bright blue eyes and a smile that would melt the hardest of hearts.

We had the same interests. Films, music, you name it. Many was the time that we would wile away the hours going through my record collection. Many was the excuse so that I could run over the hill with a couple of videos or records just for the chance of a chat.

That same year I moved away and we lost touch although. Later when I came back to Worcester I bumped into her again but it was only a quick chat and then we both went on our way again.

Relations with my parents were ok and we saw each other from time to time. Mostly it was when they went to Port Isaac for a visit. And so now you must be thinking to yourself, eh?

Having explained earlier. From 1985 until 2002, I did not have a life. Drifting from this to that and not really in control of anything. Used and abused by people on a daily basis - that's 17 years that need to simply be wiped clean. I spend no time thinking about them and have only done so this time because of the book.

The only points of note are the ones that have been mentioned. It is not a question that you have been shortchanged but there is not the time to devote to that part of my life. Maybe once this has been completed and any dust that it throws up has settled, it might find a way. Then again my wife really does not want to see anything like that down on paper. It would also not really be fair on mum and dad. I respect my wife's wishes and so all I can say is we will see. I expect that a couple of people will be upset but you cannot please everyone. There has been a story to tell. Sometimes a funny one and then sometimes upsetting. In reality, in the background my parents have always been there whether I chose to recognise it or not.

It's not easy being a parent and you do whatever it takes. Sometimes it pays to take a back seat and see how it all plays out. Sometimes it gets so bad that there is no choice but to remain in that seat.

I have seen my dad cry once and that was in the mountains of South America. My mother has never cried. I have no recollection of my mum and dad ever saying directly to me that they love me. I have no memory of them ever saying that they are proud of me.

That's ok because that is not the sort of people that they are. I know that they do and I know that they are because they tell other people. My wife for example.

In every generation you try to do it differently when you have children but it never works out like that.

If we had the solution then there would be no problems and there would be no tears. In the last three years I have been given more opportunities than I ever thought possible. I know now what has allowed my parents to have been married for over 40 years. I understand the sort of commitment it takes. My eyes have been opened and I am better for it.

Ex thief, ex junkie, ex thug ex alcoholic, ex all-round scumbag. I have been to hell. I survived.

I came back.

Nicky, Nicky, Nicky. Where o where do I start. I expect that the beginning will be just as good a place as any.

Three years ago on a lovely summer's day, a Sunday, I had been sitting with a mate yapping and having a few beers.

For no apparent reason I got up and said that I would be back in a bit. I got in my car and drove up the road. I was heading to see if Nicky still lived in the same house.

Having arrived at the house I knocked on the door and waited. I was sweating nervously. Around the corner she came from the garden. Absolutely goddamn stunning. I was at a loss and what words I did manage to get out must have sounded like absolute gibberish. After what seemed like an eternity and a few more pints of sweat I apologised for making a fool of myself and left. When I got back I explained everything to my mate and the conversation went like this. My friend speaks first.

'So, she was in when you got there.'
'Yes.'
'And she was really pleased to see you.'
'Yes'
'And no on else lives there.'
'No.'
'And you got invited in for coffee.'
'Yes.'
'And you said no.'
'Yes.'

Before he had had a chance to say any more I was back in my car and when I got there I did indeed accept that cup of coffee. We chatted and laughed long into the night and before I left we arranged to meet for coffee in the morning.

The week sped by and although it seems like a whirlwind, I moved in at the weekend. Two people know when something is right and we have talked many times about how we had never got together sooner.

Nicky's brother had been killed some years before on May 23rd. The day that I had had my thought for no reason was May 23rd.

It wasn't long before my parents met her and they got on like a house on fire. I was being allowed to be me. Nothing was expected of me and I was on a new level with my parents because of it. My wife has allowed me to become the person that I have always had inside me. We see mum and dad three or four times a year and always have a great time.

Nicky has opened my eyes to the possibilities and we have built a home together. It is a happy home full of laughter and we discuss our problems openly.

What is more she has given me back my mum and dad. Helped me to understand. I forgot to say that we got married on New Year's Eve 2003. The weather was perfect. The music was perfect. Mum and dad were there and the next day it snowed which was what Nicky wanted. I wrote her name in the snow and we had a great time.

I have literally come full circle.

I mean, who the fuck said life is a lottery. Play with the cards that you have been dealt. What a crock of shit.

My dad always told me that you do not know unless you try and that as long as you do your best then that will always be good enough.

And that's the secret. That's parenting.

Its also the recipe of a happy marriage. Make the effort and you will reap the rewards. Finally I understand all that but it took someone who loved me for me to get me to see it.

Mum and dad may not at first have seemed to be the greatest parents in the world, but they are. They belong to that rare breed that never gave up. In their own way they were always with me. They always prayed for me and they always had hope for me.

Sure I let them down but they never gave up. I am not the sort of person that has many friends because I find it very hard to trust people.

I can have discussions with mum and dad that I never thought possible. We can have such a laugh and I understand so much more. My wife has given me this and I will love her always.

I suppose this is more of a book for my dad because I have always been able to talk to my mum. They are however both equal.

I have long lived under the shadow that I would never be any good. Would never match up to my dad. Well I've gotten round that. Whereas my dad is the smartest man I know I make up for it in practical know-how.

But its not a competition. I thank them now for everything they have ever done to me for me and taught me. I thank my wife for allowing me to see that my dad is the best. Of course he is, he's my dad. My mum is an absolute diamond but I feel that I can stand shoulder to shoulder with them now as equals.

My parents are my greatest friends. My wife is my best friend.

There is more for me to learn and I am glad that there is still time to benefit from my parents' wisdom and love.

I took a journey and the road was fraught with danger. I have stared death in the face.

Looked with frightened eyes.

The demons are gone.

And finally I have found my peace. Peace with my life. Peace in my mind. And best of all?

I got my parents back.

We all have demons that need facing. I have met mine, entertained them and finally dispatched them. My wife has allowed me to see that there are better things out there and my children have allowed me to see that I am still a big kid at heart. They are all wonderful and I am fortunate that having lived the life that I did I will be a good guide to them when they all begin life's journey.

This book has been a long time coming and no doubt there are things that I have forgotten but the meaning is there nonetheless.

And so happy days are here again.

Got to go now. My wife has been on at me to write a cookery book for the last four years so having compiled various recipes of the last few decades I had better get on.

But don't worry mum I wont put any of the witches brews in it as the photos wouldn't be too appealing.

Witches brews. Whatever next?

Thinking about it, maybe just the one mother.

Maybe just the one.